LE CORDON BLEU

HOME COLLECTION

·BRUNCH·

PERIPLUS
EDITIONS

contents

recipe ratings 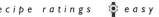 *easy* *a little more care needed* *more care needed*

Fresh fruit kebabs

Sweet fruit kebabs served hot with a little crème fraîche or yogurt make a delicious alternative to fresh fruit salad.

*Preparation time **20 minutes + at least 2 hours standing + 30 minutes marinating***
*Total cooking time **7 minutes***
Serves 4

1 teaspoon finely chopped fresh rosemary
1/3 cup honey
1 lb. mixed fresh fruit, such as strawberries, kiwi fruit, mango, apricots or pineapple
2 teaspoons sugar

1   Combine the rosemary and honey with 2 tablespoons water in a saucepan and bring slowly to a boil over low heat. Remove, cool, cover with plastic wrap and leave for 2 hours or preferably overnight in the refrigerator.
2   Soak 16 small wooden skewers, or long ones cut to 6-inch lengths, in water for at least 30 minutes. Prepare the fruit by washing and peeling as appropriate. Leave fruit such as strawberries whole, cut kiwi fruit into thick slices, mango into large chunks, halve the apricots, and so on. The fruit should roughly match in size. Thread onto the skewers, place in a shallow dish and pour the honey and rosemary over the top. Set aside for 30 minutes, brushing the kebabs occasionally with the liquid.
3   Preheat the broiler to high. Drain the fruit, reserving the liquid. Sprinkle the sugar on the fruit and broil in a shallow heatproof dish, in batches. Cook for 5–7 minutes, or until the edges are beginning to color, brushing the fruit with the honey mixture halfway through cooking. Serve hot, drizzled with the juice, and with some crème fraîche or yogurt on the side, if desired.

Chef's tip Dried fruit can be used. Mix in a saucepan with the prepared honey and rosemary, heat for 2 minutes, cool and thread onto skewers. Broil for 3 minutes.

Swiss muesli

A light, healthy start to the day, this homemade granola makes use of a variety of fruits and nuts according to what is readily available.

*Preparation time **10 minutes***
*Total cooking time **10 minutes***
Serves 1

1 tablespoon raisins
2/3 cup thick plain yogurt
1 tablespoon honey
1/4 cup rolled oats
2 tablespoons almonds or hazelnuts, toasted, skinned and chopped
1 passionfruit
1 small mango, cubed, or 1 banana, sliced, reserving a few pieces for decoration
a few extra toasted almonds, to garnish

1   Put the raisins in a small bowl, pour in boiling water to cover and set aside while preparing the muesli.
2   In a small bowl, stir the yogurt, honey, rolled oats and nuts together.
3   With a small sharp knife, halve the passionfruit. Using a teaspoon, scoop out the seeds and pulp and add to the yogurt mixture. Drain the raisins and add them to the mixture with the mango or banana. Mix gently until just combined.
4   Spoon into a bowl and decorate with the reserved fruit and the almonds.

Chef's tips If you like a sweeter muesli, drizzle with a little extra honey or Demerara sugar before eating.

Fresh fruits of the season such as strawberries, peaches, pears or any others of your choice can also be used.

Fresh fruit kebabs (top) and Swiss muesli

Broiled grapefruit

How luxurious to be presented with a perfectly prepared grapefruit! Refreshing and tangy, these make an interesting starter for breakfast or brunch.

Preparation time **20 minutes**
Total cooking time **5 minutes**
Serves 4

2 large grapefruit, preferably pink
2 teaspoons Cointreau
4 teaspoons Demerara sugar
pinch of nutmeg

1 Halve the grapefruit through the equator and cut a thin sliver from the base of each so that each half will sit without tipping over. Using the point of a grapefruit knife, cut down each side of every membrane to loosen the segments. Be careful not to cut through the skin.
2 Still using the grapefruit knife, loosen the fruit from the sides and the base by cutting around where the flesh meets the white pith. If you want an even better result, remove the membrane by gently holding the segments down with the knife and pulling the membrane up towards the center. Take hold of it and carefully pull it out with the central pithy core, leaving the segments neatly in position.
3 Drain off any excess juice and place the grapefruit on a heatproof tray or broiler pan. Pour 1/2 teaspoon Cointreau on each half of grapefruit. Preheat the broiler to a high temperature. Mix the sugar with the nutmeg and sprinkle over the grapefruit. Immediately place the grapefruit under the broiler to heat through and lightly brown the surface. Serve hot on warm plates.

Chef's tip Steps 1 and 2 may be done the day before. Cover the grapefruit halves and refrigerate overnight.

Scrambled eggs with smoked salmon

Scrambled eggs are delicious served with toast, as a filling for croissants, or alternatively, in vol-au-vent shells. The key to making really creamy scrambled eggs is not to overcook them.

Preparation time **10 minutes**
Total cooking time **5 minutes**
Serves 4–6

1/4 lb. smoked salmon
10 eggs
1/3 cup heavy cream
1 tablespoon unsalted butter
sprigs of fresh flat-leaf parsley, to garnish

1 Set aside a few whole pieces of smoked salmon for decoration. Finely chop the rest and set aside.
2 In a bowl, whisk the eggs with the cream and season with salt and pepper.
3 Melt the butter in a skillet. Add the eggs and cook over medium heat, stirring constantly, for about 3–5 minutes, or until the eggs are thick and creamy but still have a flowing consistency. Stir in the chopped salmon and serve immediately, garnished with the whole pieces of salmon and some parsley. Serve with fingers of toast.

Chef's tips Scrambled eggs will continue cooking even when the pan is removed from the heat, so it is important that everything is ready to serve as soon as the eggs are done.

If you prefer, you can leave the salmon in whole pieces and serve it beside the eggs.

Broiled grapefruit (top) and
Scrambled eggs with smoked salmon

French toast with berry compote

To enjoy this berry compote year-round, make it with fresh or frozen berries. Any leftover compote may be used to flavor plain yogurt.

Preparation time **10 minutes**
Total cooking time **35 minutes**
Serves 4

¹/₃ cup sugar
juice of 1 lemon
1 lb. fresh or frozen strawberries, blueberries,
　　raspberries, blackberries or pitted cherries
¹/₄ cup honey
6 eggs
¹/₃ cup heavy cream
pinch of ground cinnamon
¹/₃ cup unsalted butter
8 slices of white bread
2 tablespoons confectioners' sugar

1 Combine the sugar and the lemon juice with ¹/₄ cup water in a saucepan. Heat until the sugar is dissolved. Stir in the fruit, bring to a boil, reduce the heat and simmer for 5–10 minutes, or until the fruit is soft but still whole. If using frozen fruit, use from frozen and cook it a little longer.

2 Strain the fruit and put the juice in a small saucepan with the honey. Bring to a boil, stirring well. Cook for 7–10 minutes, or until the juice coats the back of a spoon. Put the fruit in a bowl and stir the juice into the fruit.

3 In a bowl, whisk together the eggs, cream and cinnamon. Melt a quarter of the butter in a nonstick skillet over medium heat. Dip two slices of bread in the egg and cook for 2–4 minutes, or until golden on both sides. Repeat with the remaining butter and bread, keeping the cooked slices in a 300°F oven. Put two slices of the French toast on each plate, dust with sifted confectioners' sugar and serve with the fruit compote.

Eggs Benedict

Toasted English muffins topped with crisp bacon, lightly poached eggs and smothered in rich buttery hollandaise sauce. This American specialty is a truly memorable breakfast or brunch treat.

Preparation time **25 minutes**
Total cooking time **10 minutes**
Serves **4**

HOLLANDAISE SAUCE
2 egg yolks
2 tablespoons water
¹/3 cup clarified butter (see Chef's tip), melted
¹/2 teaspoon lemon juice

8 slices bacon
4 English muffins, fork-split into halves
¹/4 cup vinegar
8 eggs
4 pitted black olives, cut in half, or
    8 slices of truffle

1 To make the hollandaise sauce, follow the method in the Chef's techniques on page 63. Cover the surface with a disk of waxed paper and keep warm over the hot water, off the heat.

2 Broil the bacon until crisp and toast the muffins. Put the bacon on the muffins and keep them warm.
3 To make the poached eggs, half-fill a large skillet with water and bring to a boil. Reduce the temperature to low and add the vinegar. The water should be barely at simmering point.
4 Crack the eggs one at a time into a small cup or bowl and carefully slide them into the vinegared water two or three at a time. Cook for 2–3 minutes, or until the egg whites are firm but not hard. Very gently remove the eggs, using a slotted spoon, and drain well.
5 Immediately top each muffin and bacon with a poached egg. Cover with the hollandaise sauce, decorate with the olive halves and serve.

Chef's tip You will need about 3/4 cup butter to yield 1/3 cup clarified butter. Melt the butter gently over low heat in a small heavy-bottomed saucepan, without stirring or shaking the pan. Skim the froth from the top, then pour the clear butter into another container, leaving the white sediment in the base of the pan. Cover and keep in the refrigerator for up to 4 weeks.

Rösti with bacon

*This recipe allows you to use potatoes that have already been cooked,
making a quick and delicious dish.*

*Preparation time **15 minutes***
*Total cooking time **45 minutes***
Serves 6

3–4 waxy potatoes
4 thin slices bacon
2 tablespoons oil
2 tablespoons unsalted butter
1 onion, thinly sliced

1 Preheat the oven to 350°F. Scrub the unpeeled potatoes and put them in a saucepan. Cover with cold water, add salt, and bring to a boil. Reduce the heat and simmer for 10 minutes. Drain and allow the potatoes to cool completely. Meanwhile, fry the bacon in a hot dry skillet or broil until crisp. Remove and chop or break into bite-size pieces.

2 Peel the potatoes and either cut into fine sticks or coarsely shred them into a bowl. Add the bacon. In a large nonstick skillet, heat 1 tablespoon oil and add the butter. Gently cook the onion until soft and transparent.

Add to the potatoes and bacon, season with salt and pepper and mix until combined.

3 To make individual rösti, spoon the mixture into greased egg rings placed in a lightly oiled, heavy-bottomed skillet. Press down with the back of a spoon or spatula. Brown the first side over medium heat for 5–7 minutes. Turn each rösti over, using a spatula, and put them back in the pan brown-side-up, being careful not to break up the potato. Cook the rösti for another 5 minutes, to crisp the bottom.

4 To make one large rösti, put the mixture into a large nonstick ovenproof skillet greased with 2 teaspoons oil and brown the underneath over high heat. Transfer the pan to the oven for 15 minutes. Remove, then flip the rösti by turning it out onto a plate and carefully sliding it back into the pan. Add the remaining oil to the pan if necessary. Return the pan to the oven for 10 minutes. Turn the rösti out onto a plate and serve whole or cut into slices.

Chef's tip If you prefer plain rösti, omit the bacon and serve with slices of crispy bacon on the side.

Salmon kedgeree

An old English favorite with a twist: fresh salmon and dill replace the traditional smoked haddock. Prepare the ingredients the day before.

Preparation time **20 minutes**
Total cooking time **16 minutes**
Serves 4

2 eggs, at room temperature
3 tablespoons unsalted butter
3/4 lb. salmon fillet, cooked and flaked
1 1/4 cups raw long-grain rice, cooked and well drained
1 egg, beaten
1/4 cup whipping cream
1–2 teaspoons chopped fresh dill weed or snipped fresh chives

1 Bring a small saucepan of water to a boil, gently put in the two eggs, return to a boil and simmer for 7 minutes. Remove with a spoon and place in a bowl of iced water to cool. Tap the shells with the back of a spoon to craze them, then peel. Coarsely chop the eggs on a plate. The yolks should still be a little moist.
2 Melt the butter in a skillet, add the salmon and heat for 30 seconds. Add the rice and the chopped egg and, using a wide spatula, toss over high heat for 2 minutes, or until hot. Keep your movements light and the mixture loose; you do not want to compact the rice.
3 Add the beaten egg with the cream. Continue to toss for 3–5 minutes, scraping the base of the pan, until the egg has set. Season to taste with salt and pepper. Pile onto a warm serving dish and scatter with the fresh dill weed or chives to serve.

Chef's tips For the best result, the rice needs to be as dry as possible, so cook it the day before, drain it well, cover and refrigerate.

Don't worry that the boiled eggs initially seem underdone as they will continue to cook in the kedgeree.

Basic crêpes

Thin, lacy pancakes made using this traditional batter may be cooked in advance and kept overnight in the refrigerator or frozen for later use.

Preparation time **5 minutes + 30 minutes resting**
Total cooking time **40 minutes**
Makes **12**

3/4 cup all-purpose flour
1/2 teaspoon salt
3 eggs, lightly beaten
1 egg yolk
2/3 cup milk
1 1/2 tablespoons oil or melted clarified butter

1 Sift the flour and salt into a bowl. Make a well in the center, drop in the eggs and yolk and mix with a wooden spoon or whisk, mixing in a little at a time. Combine the milk with 1/4 cup water and gradually add until all the flour is incorporated. Beat in the oil or butter until smooth. Cover and let rest at room temperature for 30 minutes.
2 Melt a little oil or clarified butter in a shallow, heavy-bottomed or nonstick skillet, 8 inches in diameter, until almost smoking, then pour off any excess. This will leave a fine coating—enough to cook one crêpe. From a measuring cup or ladle, pour in a small amount of batter, swirling the pan to coat just the bottom with a thin layer. Cook for 1–2 minutes, or until the edges are brown. Loosen around the edge with a round-bladed knife and turn or flip the crêpe and cook for another 1–2 minutes. Turn out onto waxed paper. Repeat with the remaining batter. Stack the crêpes with a piece of waxed paper between each, then cover to prevent drying out. Serve sprinkled with lemon juice and sugar.

Chef's tip To store, stack the crêpes and wrap in foil. Seal in a plastic bag to refrigerate overnight or freeze for up to 3 months. Defrost in the refrigerator overnight.

Crêpes jubilee

Thin light pancakes rolled around a black cherry filling enhanced with lemon, cinnamon and Kirsch.

Preparation time **10 minutes**
Total cooking time **10 minutes**
Serves **6–8**

1 quantity basic crêpes
2 x 16 oz. cans pitted black cherries
finely grated rind of 1 lemon
1 cinnamon stick or 1/4 teaspoon ground cinnamon
4 teaspoons cornstarch
1/3 cup confectioners' sugar
1 tablespoon Kirsch
2 tablespoons unsalted butter, melted
confectioners' sugar, to dust

1 To prepare the filling, drain the cherries and pour the juice into a small saucepan. Add the lemon rind and cinnamon and slowly bring to a boil. Remove from the heat. In a bowl, mix the cornstarch with a little water to make a paste and pour in half the hot juice. Blend well, stir it into the juice in the pan, return the pan to the heat and stir until boiling. Reduce the heat, remove the cinnamon stick, add the cherries, confectioners' sugar and Kirsch, and heat gently until the cherries are just warmed through.
2 Preheat the oven to 325°F. Spoon some of the cherry mixture into the center of each crêpe and roll up like a cigar. Place in a baking dish in a single layer, brush with the melted butter and heat through in the oven for 5 minutes. Dust with some sifted confectioners' sugar and serve.

Chef's tip The filling for these crêpes can be varied. Chopped apricots or peaches can be used instead of the cherries, and you can use amaretto instead of Kirsch. If the crêpes have been prepared in advance and are still chilled, reheat for 10 minutes, covered with foil.

Basic crêpes (bottom) and Crêpes jubilee

Brunch crêpe stack

This stack can be prepared the day before. The egg white, however, must be whisked and folded in at the last moment. Experiment by creating your own fillings for the layers or even using up leftovers.

Preparation time 25 minutes
Total cooking time 1 hour 45 minutes
Serves 4–6

TOMATO FILLING
2 tablespoons unsalted butter
1 shallot, finely chopped
1 teaspoon paprika
2 teaspoons tomato paste
6–7 tomatoes, halved, seeded and
    coarsely chopped
small pinch of sugar

MUSHROOM FILLING
2 tablespoons unsalted butter
1 shallot, finely chopped
1 1/2 cups chopped button mushrooms
1 teaspoon all-purpose flour
1/4 cup milk
1 tablespoon chopped fresh parsley
small pinch of ground nutmeg

HAM FILLING
2/3 cup finely chopped ham (or chopped
    cooked bacon, sausages or chicken)
1 teaspoon French mustard
1 tablespoon chutney

1 tablespoon unsalted butter
1 tablespoon all-purpose flour
3/4 cup milk
1 egg, separated
1/4 cup shredded strong Cheddar
1 tablespoon grated Parmesan
7 thin crêpes (see page 16)

1 To prepare the tomato filling, melt the butter in a saucepan, add the shallot, cover and cook for 4–5 minutes, or until transparent. Stir in the paprika for 1 minute, add the tomato paste and stir over low heat for another minute. Add the tomatoes and sugar, season, and simmer for about 45 minutes, or until thick. Cover and set aside.

2 To make the mushroom filling, melt the butter in a skillet, add the shallot, cover and cook for 4–5 minutes, or until transparent. Add the mushrooms and cook until dry. Remove from the heat and stir in the flour and milk. Return to a low heat and stir constantly until the liquid is smooth and begins to thicken. Increase the heat and stir as the mixture comes to a boil. Simmer for 1 minute, remove from the stove and stir in the parsley, nutmeg, salt and pepper. Cover and set aside.

3 To prepare the ham filling, mix together all the ingredients in a small bowl. Set aside.

4 Melt the butter in a saucepan, add the flour off the heat and stir for 1 minute. Pour in the milk, whisk to blend and return to the stove over low heat. Stir constantly until the mixture is smooth and begins to thicken, then increase the heat and bring to a boil. Remove from the stove. Stir in the egg yolk and half the Cheddar and Parmesan. Season, cover and set side.

5 Preheat the oven to 400°F. Butter a round ovenproof dish or pie plate about 10–11 inches across the base. Put a crêpe on the base and spread with half the ham filling. Cover with another crêpe and spread with half the mushroom filling, cover with a third crêpe and spoon over half the tomato filling. Repeat with the rest of the crêpes and fillings. Top with a final crêpe, brownest-side-up.

6 To finish, whisk the egg white and fold it into the cheese sauce. Spoon over the stack (a little may go over the edge) sprinkle with the remaining cheese and bake for 15 minutes, or until golden. Cut into six portions.

Bagels

Whether plain or sprinkled with sesame or poppy seeds, these yeasted bread rolls, characteristic of Jewish baking, are delicious served warm with butter. The traditional shiny, hard crust is achieved by boiling the bagels before baking them. See page 63 for step-by-step instructions to accompany this recipe.

*Preparation time **50 minutes + 1 hour proving***
*Total cooking time **25 minutes***
Makes 12 large or 24 small bagels

1/2 oz. (2 tablespoons) dried yeast
2 tablespoons oil
2 teaspoons salt
3 tablespoons sugar
4 cups bread or all-purpose flour
1 egg, beaten, for glazing

1 Dissolve the yeast in 1 cup lukewarm water, then add the oil.
2 Combine the salt, sugar and flour, then make a well in the center. Add the yeast mixture and gradually incorporate the flour until a dough forms. Continue working the dough until the sides of the bowl come clean. Knead the dough for 10 minutes, then shape it into a ball and place in the bottom of the bowl.

Cover with a moist towel and set aside in a warm place to rise for about 30–45 minutes, or until double in size. Line two baking trays with waxed paper.
3 Once the dough has doubled in size, punch it down and knead for 8–10 minutes, then divide into 12 or 24 pieces. Roll them into tight balls. Poke a finger through the center of each ball and gently enlarge the hole until the dough resembles a doughnut. Place on a floured baking sheet, cover with a moist towel and let rise again for 15 minutes. Preheat the oven to 400°F.
4 In the meantime, bring a large saucepan of water to a simmer. Cook the bagels in the water for 1–2 minutes on each side, then remove and place on the lined baking sheets. Allow to cool for 5 minutes. Brush each bagel with beaten egg and bake for 20–25 minutes, or until golden brown.

Chef's tip Once the bagels have been brushed with the egg, they can be sprinkled with poppy seeds or sesame seeds before baking.

Eggs en cocotte with smoked trout and leek

Eggs that are en cocotte *are baked in the oven in ramekins placed in a* bain-marie. *An excellent breakfast dish, these eggs would also make a wonderful first course.*

Preparation time **15 minutes**
Total cooking time **35 minutes**
Serves 4

3 tablespoons unsalted butter
I small leek, halved and thinly sliced
6 oz. smoked trout, flaked finely
1/2 cup whipping cream
4 eggs
I teaspoon snipped fresh chives

1 Melt the butter in a saucepan. Add the leek, cover and cook gently for 8 minutes, or until soft but not brown. Meanwhile, brush four small (2/3-cup) ovenproof ramekins or soufflé dishes with a little melted butter.

2 Remove the leek from the heat and stir in the trout and a third of the cream. Season, spoon into the dishes and allow to cool. The cocottes can be prepared up to this stage the night before, covered and refrigerated.

3 Preheat the oven to 325°F. With the back of a teaspoon, make a slight indentation in the center of the mixture in each of the dishes. Break an egg into each cocotte, spoon a tablespoon of cream on each and sprinkle with salt and pepper and 2 teaspoons of the chives. Place the dishes in a baking dish or roasting pan and pour in enough boiling water to come halfway up the sides.

4 Bake for 20–25 minutes, or until the whites are set and the yolks are cooked but still tremble when lightly shaken. Set each cocotte on a cold plate, sprinkle with the remaining chives and serve immediately with fingers of freshly made buttered toast.

Frittata

Unlike a French omelet, the Italian frittata usually requires all ingredients to be mixed with the eggs before being cooked to a fairly firm texture.

Preparation time **20 minutes**
Total cooking time **30 minutes**
Serves 4–6

1/4 lb. skinless, boneless chicken breast halves
1/4 cup unsalted butter
1 1/3 cups sliced button mushrooms
2 cloves garlic, chopped
I red bell pepper, sliced into short strips
10 eggs, beaten and seasoned with salt and pepper
I cup shredded Gruyère or Cheddar cheese

1 Preheat the oven to 425°F.

2 Cut the chicken breast into small 1/2-inch cubes and season with salt and pepper. Melt the butter in an ovenproof skillet over medium heat. Once the butter has melted, cook the chicken for 2–3 minutes, until lightly browned.

3 Add the mushrooms and cook for 5–7 minutes, or until any liquid has evaporated. Add the garlic and red pepper. Season with salt and pepper and cover. Lower the heat and cook gently for 5–8 minutes, or until the red pepper is tender.

4 Add the beaten eggs and stir to distribute evenly. Continue stirring for about 2–3 minutes, or until the eggs begin to set.

5 Sprinkle the cheese over the eggs and transfer the skillet to the oven. Cook for 5–8 minutes, or until the cheese has melted and the eggs are cooked through. Remove from the oven and slide the frittata onto a plate. Cut into wedges to serve.

Eggs en cocotte with smoked trout and leek (top) and Frittata

Coffee granita with panna cotta

A coffee-flavored granita teamed with a silky
Italian custard makes a refreshing start to the day.

Preparation time ***1 hour + overnight chilling***
Total cooking time ***20 minutes***
Serves 4

I cup sugar
¹/4 cup instant dark-roast coffee powder
2 tablespoons coffee liqueur, optional
2 teaspoons powdered gelatin
2 vanilla beans, split lengthways
I cup milk
I cup heavy cream

1 Simmer 3/4 cup water and 3/4 cup of the sugar in a saucepan for 10 minutes. Mix the coffee with a little water to form a paste, stir in and allow to cool.
2 Add 2 cups water and the liqueur. Pour the granita into a shallow plastic or metal container and allow to freeze overnight.
3 Dissolve the gelatin powder in 2 tablespoons cold water. Scrape the vanilla seeds into a saucepan and add the beans, milk, cream and remaining sugar. Bring to a boil, strain into a bowl and discard the beans.
4 Add the gelatin to the hot milk mixture, then stir to melt. Place the bowl inside a bowl of ice water and stir until the gelatin begins to set (as the spoon is drawn through it, you will see a line across the base of the bowl). Pour into four small (2/3-cup) gelatin molds or ramekins. Chill overnight.
5 Half an hour before serving, refrigerate four plates. Release the panna cotta from the molds by wrapping in a hot cloth and turning over. Scoop out the granita in flakes by drawing the side of a metal spoon across its surface. Serve on the chilled plates with the panna cotta.

Caramelized onion, spinach and blue cheese quiche

The delicious combination of vegetables with blue cheese and a hint of nutmeg
makes a perfect filling for this vegetarian quiche.

Preparation time **30 minutes + 50 minutes refrigeration**
Total cooking time **1 hour 45 minutes**
Serves 8–10

PASTRY
1²/3 cups all-purpose flour
1 teaspoon salt
1/3 cup unsalted butter, chilled and cubed
1 egg, lightly beaten

FILLING
2 tablespoons vegetable oil
4 onions, thinly sliced
1 teaspoon sugar
1/3 cup red wine
3 tablespoons unsalted butter
10 oz. frozen spinach, thawed and squeezed dry
pinch of ground nutmeg
3/4 cup heavy cream
6 oz. strong blue cheese, such as Roquefort or Stilton
4 eggs, beaten

1 Brush a 9¹/2 x 1¹/4-inch fluted tart pan with removable base with melted butter. Sift together the flour and salt into a large bowl, add the butter and, using a fast, light flicking action of the thumb across the tips of the fingers, rub into the flour until the mixture resembles fine bread crumbs. Make a well in the center and pour in the egg and 2 teaspoons water. Mix together to make a rough ball. Turn out onto a lightly floured surface and knead very gently for 20 seconds until just smooth, place in plastic wrap and chill for at least 20 minutes.

2 Roll out the pastry on a floured surface to a circle approximately 1/8-inch thick. Fold half the pastry over the rolling pin and lift into the pan. Push into the sides of the pan by using a small ball of lightly floured excess pastry. Trim off any excess pastry with a sharp knife or roll over the top of the pan with the rolling pin. Refrigerate for 30 minutes. Preheat the oven to 350°F.

3 Cut a circle of waxed paper 1¹/4 inches larger than the tart pan, crush it into a ball to soften, then open and lay inside the pastry shell so that it comes up the sides. Fill with pie weights or rice, then press down gently and bake for 10 minutes, or until firm. Remove the weights or rice and discard the paper. Return the pastry to the oven and continue to bake for 5–10 minutes, or until the pastry is dry. Remove and cool. Raise the oven temperature to 375°F.

4 For the filling, heat the oil in a large saucepan. Add the onions and cook gently for 8 minutes, or until translucent. Raise the heat, add the sugar and cook for 5–10 minutes, or until the onions begin to caramelize. Next, pour in the wine and cook until the liquid has evaporated and the onions are soft. Season with salt and pepper. Remove from the pan and set aside.

5 In the pan, melt the butter, add the spinach and fry over high heat, stirring constantly, until the spinach is dry when pressed with the back of a spoon. (Wet spinach will make the quiche soggy.) Season with salt, pepper and the nutmeg, turn out onto a chopping board and chop finely.

6 In a saucepan, warm the cream and cheese gently, stirring, until the cheese melts, but does not boil. Season and cool before adding the eggs. Fill the pastry shell with the onion, then the spinach. Smooth the surface a little but do not pack down. Pour in the cream mixture and bake for 30 minutes, then lower the temperature to 325°F and bake for 20 minutes to cook the center of the quiche. Cover with foil if it is getting too brown. Serve warm.

Brie purses with pears and almonds

A sophisticated brunch dish which may be served with broiled tomatoes, some watercress or a green salad.
This would also make an elegant first course for a lunch or dinner party.

Preparation time **25 minutes + 30 minutes chilling**
Total cooking time **15 minutes**
Serves 4

3/4 cup whole blanched almonds
1 large or 2 small ripe pears, peeled and thinly sliced
2 tablespoons balsamic or tarragon vinegar
1/2 lb. ripe Brie
12 sheets phyllo pastry
2/3 cup unsalted butter, melted

1 Preheat a broiler to a high heat. Place the almonds in a food processor and blend for 30 seconds, or until they resemble fine bread crumbs. Turn out onto a baking sheet and place under the broiler to toast. Do not walk away while this is happening as the almonds will burn very quickly. Season the toasted almonds with a little salt and pepper.

2 Place the pear slices in a bowl and sprinkle with the vinegar, toss to coat well and set aside. Cut the Brie in half through the middle to make two large flat pieces with a rind on one side of each. Lay one piece on a work surface, rind downwards, and place the pear slices on top of the cheese in a neat layer to completely cover the top of the cheese. You may need to do several layers in

order to use up all the pears. Sprinkle with any remaining vinegar, season with salt and pepper and place the second piece of Brie on top, so that the rind is uppermost and the edges are even all the way around. Wrap the cheese tightly in plastic wrap, place on a plate and chill for a minimum of 30 minutes. When chilled, cut into eight evenly sized pieces and coat them with the almonds, taking care to keep the wedges whole.

3 Preheat the oven to 425°F. Brush one sheet of phyllo with the melted butter, cover with another sheet, brush again, then add a third sheet. Cut into two 8-inch squares. Discard the trimmings. Place one wedge of the Brie in the center of each square and gather up the edges to form a purse, squeezing the pastry together to make a "drawstring" effect. Brush gently with a little more butter. Repeat this process with the remaining pastry and Brie, making sure the Brie remains chilled or it will melt too quickly. When ready to cook, place the purses on a greased baking sheet and bake for 10 minutes, or until golden. Serve immediately.

Chef's tip A few ripe, peeled and sliced apricots or peeled seedless grapes can be used instead of the pears, or if time is limited, omit both the fruit and the vinegar and spread the opened-out cheese with 2 tablespoons of a fruit chutney instead.

Eastern rice pudding

The cardamom adds a distinctly Eastern flavor to this creamy rice pudding. Try serving it with the spicy fig preserves on page 51.

Preparation time **5 minutes**
Total cooking time **25 minutes**
Serves **4**

seeds of 4 cardamom pods, crushed
1 1/2 cups cream
1 3/4 cups milk
1/3 cup sugar
1/3 cup short-grain rice

1 Combine the crushed cardamom pods, the cream and the milk in a medium saucepan. Bring to a boil, remove from the heat, cool slightly and stir in the sugar and rice. At this stage, the rice mixture can be refrigerated overnight or it can be cooked immediately.
2 Bring the rice mixture to a boil, lower the heat and cook, stirring constantly as it begins to thicken, for 20–25 minutes, or until the rice is just soft and the liquid has become creamy. The pudding should have a soft, flowing consistency and when a spoon is drawn through, the bottom of the pan should be seen and the pudding flow quickly to fill the parting behind it. (Remember that the rice will continue to thicken slightly when removed from the heat.) Serve with dried fruits or a fruit preserve.

Rhubarb with ginger

This tangy rhubarb compote is enhanced by the color and flavor of the red currant jelly and enlivened by the ginger.

Preparation time **10 minutes**
Total cooking time **20 minutes**
Serves **4**

1/4 cup red currant jelly
2 lb. fresh rhubarb
2 tablespoons rinsed and finely chopped crystallized or preserved ginger
a little granulated white sugar or Demerara sugar

1 In a small bowl, beat the red currant jelly with a spoon until smooth, pour into a wide saucepan and add 1/3 cup water.
2 Trim and discard the leaves and the base of the stalks from the rhubarb. Cut the rhubarb into 1-inch slices and add to the pan in a single layer.
3 Bring to a boil and immediately turn the heat down to a bare simmer. Cover tightly with a lid or foil and cook for 10–15 minutes, or until tender. The rhubarb should still hold its shape. Be careful to cook very gently or you will end up with a purée.
4 Transfer to a bowl, add the ginger and taste. You may require a little white or Demerara sugar sprinkled over at this stage, depending on the acidity of the rhubarb. Allow to cool slightly and serve warm or, if you prefer, prepare the day before and chill overnight.

Chef's tip The acidity of the rhubarb will vary considerably, so the recipe is only a guide as to sweetness. Add as much sugar as you require. Serve the rhubarb by itself or with thick yogurt.

Eastern rice pudding (top left) and
Rhubarb with ginger

Puff pastries with asparagus and mushrooms in creamy sauce

An ideal brunch dish: crisp in texture, the pastry is filled with subtle flavors
that come together harmoniously in a creamy sauce.

*Preparation time **30 minutes + 20 minutes chilling***
*Total cooking time **25 minutes***
Makes 6

15 asparagus spears, trimmed
2 sheets pre-rolled frozen puff pastry, thawed
1 egg, beaten
3 tablespoons unsalted butter
1/4 cup all-purpose flour
1 cup milk
1/4 cup crème fraîche or whipping cream
2³/4 cups thickly sliced button or oyster mushrooms
melted butter, for brushing

1 Bring a saucepan of salted water to a boil. Add the asparagus spears and cook for 4 minutes, or until tender. Remove from the pan, plunge into a bowl of iced water, drain well and set aside.

2 Stack the pastry sheets on a lightly floured surface and roll out to a rectangle about 12 x 8 inches. With a large sharp knife, trim to straighten the two long sides and cut into two long strips. Now cut each strip into three diamonds or squares. Place them slightly apart on a damp baking sheet and chill for 20 minutes.

3 Meanwhile, preheat the oven to 400°F. Brush the top surface of the pastry with the beaten egg. Do not brush the edges of the pastry because the egg will set and prevent the pastry from rising. Lightly score the tops of the pastry shapes in a crisscross pattern with a thin knife. Bake for about 10 minutes, or until well risen, crisp and golden. Split in half horizontally with a sharp knife. Scrape out and discard any soft dough.

4 In a medium saucepan, melt 2 tablespoons of the butter, add the flour and cook for 1 minute over low heat. Remove from the heat, pour in the milk and blend thoroughly with a wooden spoon or whisk. Return to low-medium heat, stir briskly until boiling and simmer for 2 minutes, stirring constantly. Add the crème fraîche or cream and stir over the heat for another minute. Remove from the stove and cover with foil. In a skillet, melt the remaining butter and toss the mushrooms over medium heat for 2 minutes, or until cooked. Trim the asparagus tips to 2¹/2-inch lengths and reserve. Cut the remainder of the tender stalks into 3/4-inch lengths. Add the mushrooms and the small pieces of asparagus to the sauce and mix together briefly.

5 To assemble the pastries, spoon the warm sauce onto the six pastry bases and place the asparagus tips on top. Brush them with a little melted butter and replace the pastry lids. Warm through in the oven at 325°F for 5 minutes before serving.

Chef's tips The pastry can be baked, split and scraped out the day before. Reheat in a 300°F oven before adding the filling.

Note that you may have a little of the mushroom mixture left over after filling the pastries, depending on the size of asparagus you use. This is delicious eaten on toast as a snack.

Chocolate muffins

These rich dark chocolate muffins freeze very well—simply allow to cool completely and seal in airtight freezer containers or bags for up to 3 months. To serve, thaw at room temperature and reheat.

Preparation time **10 minutes**
Total cooking time **25 minutes**
Makes 12

1²/3 **cups all-purpose flour**
¹/3 **cup unsweetened cocoa**
2/3 **cup sugar**
2 **teaspoons baking powder**
1 **cup milk**
¹/4 **cup unsalted butter, melted**
¹/4 **teaspoon vanilla extract**
3/4 **cup semisweet chocolate chips**

1 Preheat the oven to 350°F. Prepare a 12-cup standard muffin pan by greasing well or lining with paper bake cups.
2 Sift together the flour, cocoa powder, sugar, baking powder and a pinch of salt into a bowl.
3 In a small bowl, mix together the milk, melted butter and vanilla.
4 Make a well in the center of the dry ingredients and pour in the milk mixture. Stir until the liquid is just barely mixed in. The batter is supposed to be lumpy so do not overmix.
5 Gently fold in the chocolate chips. Place the mixture in the prepared muffin cups, filling each three-quarters full. Bake for 20–25 minutes, or until a tooth pick inserted into the center of a muffin comes out clean. Unmold and cool on a wire rack. Serve warm or cold.

Bacon and cheese cornbread

These individual cornbreads are quick to prepare and taste delicious served warm. As an alternative, try serving with a bowl of hearty soup for lunch on a cold winter's day.

Preparation time **20 minutes**
Total cooking time **20 minutes**
Makes 12

1 **cup yellow cornmeal**
1 **cup all-purpose flour**
2 **tablespoons sugar**
1 **teaspoon baking powder**
1 **teaspoon salt**
1¹/4 **cups buttermilk**
2 **eggs**
¹/4 **cup melted unsalted butter**
1 **cup cubed Cheddar cheese**
3–4 **slices bacon, cooked and diced**

1 Preheat the oven to 350°F. Prepare a 12-cup standard muffin pan by greasing well or lining with paper bake cups.
2 Sift together the cornmeal, flour, sugar, baking powder and salt into a bowl.
3 In a separate bowl, whisk together the buttermilk, eggs and melted butter. Make a well in the center of the dry ingredients and pour in the buttermilk mixture. Mix until just barely combined. Add the diced cheese and bacon and fold in. The batter should be thick and lumpy—do not overmix.
4 Place the mixture in the prepared pan, filling the cups three-quarters full. Bake for 15–20 minutes, or until lightly colored and a tooth pick inserted into the center of a muffin comes out clean. Unmold immediately and cool on a wire rack.

Chocolate muffins (top) and Bacon and cheese cornbread

Eggs Florentine

A classic dish made from a layer of spinach and lightly poached eggs topped with a creamy cheese sauce. For perfect poached eggs, use the freshest eggs possible.

Preparation time **25 minutes**
Total cooking time **30 minutes**
Serves 4

MORNAY SAUCE
1 tablespoon unsalted butter
2¹/₂ tablespoons all-purpose flour
1 cup milk
pinch of ground nutmeg
¹/₃ cup shredded Gruyère cheese
2 egg yolks

¹/₄ cup unsalted butter
1 lb. young spinach leaves, cleaned
¹/₄ cup vinegar
8 very fresh eggs

1 To make the mornay sauce, melt the butter in a heavy-bottomed saucepan over medium-low heat. Sprinkle the flour over the butter and cook for 1–2 minutes without allowing it to color, stirring constantly with a wooden spoon. Remove the pan from the heat and slowly add the milk, whisking or beating vigorously to avoid lumps. Return to medium heat and bring to a boil, stirring constantly. Simmer for 3–4 minutes, or until the sauce coats the back of a spoon. Stir in the nutmeg, then remove from the heat. Set aside, covered, and keep warm.

2 In a large skillet, melt the butter over low heat and add the spinach. Cook for about 5–8 minutes, or until dry. Set aside and keep warm.

3 Whisk the cheese into the mornay sauce, then whisk in the egg yolks. Season to taste, with salt and pepper. Place over low heat and mix until the cheese is melted, then heat until very hot but not boiling. Set aside, cover the surface with a piece of waxed paper and keep warm.

4 Half-fill a large skillet with water and bring to a boil over high heat. Reduce the temperature to low and add the vinegar. The water should be barely simmering.

5 Crack the eggs one at a time into a cup or bowl and carefully slide into the vinegared water two or three at a time. Cook for 2–3 minutes, or until the egg whites are firm but not hard. Very gently remove, using a slotted spoon and drain thoroughly.

6 Divide the cooked spinach evenly among four warmed plates. Place two poached eggs in the center of each mound of spinach and cover with the hot mornay sauce. Serve immediately.

Chef's tip Mornay sauce is a béchamel, or white sauce, flavored with cheese and enriched with egg yolks.

Spinach and crab roulade

Thick slices of light spinach roulade with a creamy crab filling are perfect for brunch,
a light lunch or served as a first course.

Preparation time **45 minutes**
Total cooking time **40 minutes**
Serves 6

FILLING
1 tablespoon unsalted butter
1 tablespoon all-purpose flour
3/4 cup milk
7 oz. white crab meat, fresh, frozen or canned
pinch of cayenne pepper

ROULADE
1 lb. young spinach, large stalks removed
1 tablespoon unsalted butter, melted
4 eggs, separated
pinch of ground nutmeg

1 To make the filling, melt the butter in a heavy-bottomed saucepan over low-medium heat. Sprinkle the flour over the butter and cook for 1 minute without allowing it to color, stirring constantly with a wooden spoon. Remove the pan from the heat and slowly add the milk, whisking or beating vigorously to avoid lumps. Return to low heat and briskly stir with a wooden spoon or whisk until the mixture is smooth and begins to thicken, then turn up the heat and stir briskly until boiling. Simmer for 3–4 minutes, or until the sauce coats the back of a spoon. Cover with a piece of buttered waxed paper pressed onto the surface and set aside.

2 To make the roulade, line a jelly roll pan, about 151/2 x 101/2 inches, with waxed paper. To cook the spinach, half-fill a large saucepan with water and bring to a boil, add a generous pinch of salt and the spinach. Return to a boil and cook for 1–2 minutes, then drain in a strainer, run under cold water and squeeze out the excess water. Chop finely, using a large sharp knife. Put the spinach in a large bowl and add the butter.

3 Preheat the oven to 400°F. Stir the egg yolks and nutmeg into the spinach and season well. In a large bowl, beat the egg whites until stiff and standing in peaks, then stir a large tablespoon of egg whites into the spinach mixture to lighten it. Add the remaining egg whites in one addition, then using a large metal spoon, carefully fold into the spinach. Pour into the prepared pan, lightly smoothing it to the edges with a palette knife. Bake for about 10 minutes, or until the mixture is just set and springs back to the light touch of a finger. Meanwhile, spread a clean towel onto the work surface and cover it with waxed paper.

4 Reheat the filling mixture, then stir in the crab, cayenne pepper and salt and freshly ground black pepper to taste, and heat through.

5 Turn the spinach roulade out onto the paper and towel and remove the pan and the lining paper. Quickly spread with the crab filling then, with the shortest edge towards you, pick up the towel and the paper and push the roulade away from you, holding it very low, so that the roulade rolls up like a jelly roll. Stop when the last of the roulade is underneath, then lift it onto a dish. Cut into thick slices and serve immediately.

Chef's tips This is perfect to serve alone, but can also be served with a sauce such as hollandaise or Béarnaise.

For best results, use parchment paper available at gourmet stores.

Twice-baked individual cheese soufflés

A soufflé with a difference—you can relax! Prepare these individual soufflés the day before and watch them rise again ready to thrill your brunch guests.

Preparation time **35 minutes + cooling time**
Total cooking time **45 minutes**
Serves **8**

1 1/4 cups milk
tiny pinch of grated nutmeg
1 small bay leaf
1 small shallot, halved
4 whole peppercorns
2 tablespoons unsalted butter
1/4 cup potato starch or 2 tablespoons all-purpose
flour mixed with 2 tablespoons cornstarch
1 tablespoon unsalted butter, cut into very
small pieces
3 eggs, separated
2/3 cup shredded Cheddar
1/4 teaspoon powdered mustard
1 egg white
2/3 cup whipping cream
3 tablespoons grated Parmesan or Gruyère cheese

1 In a small saucepan, warm the milk with the nutmeg, bay leaf, shallot and peppercorns. When bubbles form around the edge of the pan, remove from the heat.
2 Melt the butter in a large saucepan, remove from the heat and stir in the potato starch. Strain the milk and pour into the pan, blend well and return to the heat. Whisk briskly until the mixture comes to a boil.

Remove from the heat and scatter the butter pieces over the surface. Cover the pan with a lid and leave to cool slightly. Meanwhile, preheat the oven to 350°F. Lightly butter eight individual 2/3-cup soufflé dishes or custard cups.
3 Uncover the sauce and stir in the melted layer of butter, followed by the egg yolks, Cheddar, mustard, and salt and pepper, to taste. In a large bowl, beat the four egg whites until stiff. Using a large metal spoon or a spatula, stir 1 tablespoon of the egg whites into the cheese mixture to lighten it, then add the remainder all at once, carefully folding until just combined.
4 Divide the mixture among the soufflé dishes, pouring it in gently to avoid losing any volume. Place the dishes in a roasting pan or deep baking dish and pour in enough warm water to come three-quarters of the way up the sides of the dishes. Bake for 25 minutes, or until the soufflés have slightly risen and are firm to the touch. Remove from the water and leave to cool. (Cover and keep overnight in the refrigerator if you wish to prepare the night before.)
5 Just before serving, preheat the oven to 400°F. Return the soufflé dishes to their baking dish, pour some cream into each, dividing it equally, and season each one lightly. Sprinkle with Parmesan and pour warm water around to come three-quarters of the way up the sides of the dishes, as before. Bake for 10–15 minutes, or until risen and golden brown. Lift out carefully and place each dish on to a plate. Serve immediately.

Deviled kidneys with sage polenta disks

These herb and polenta disks are a modern alternative to the more usual toast when serving deviled kidneys for breakfast or brunch.

Preparation time **40 minutes + 1 hour resting**
Total cooking time **25 minutes**
Serves 4–6

SAGE POLENTA DISKS
2 1/2 cups milk
1 tablespoon unsalted butter
1 1/4 cups precooked or instant yellow cornmeal
   (polenta)
1/2 cup freshly grated Parmesan
2/3 cup finely chopped fresh sage leaves

oil, for deep-frying

DEVILED KIDNEYS
8 lamb kidneys
2 tablespoons tomato chutney
1/2 teaspoon mustard
dash of Worcestershire sauce
small pinch of cayenne pepper
1/4 cup unsalted butter
1 shallot, chopped
1/4 cup beef or vegetable stock

1 To prepare the sage polenta disks, heat the milk and butter in a large saucepan until nearly boiling. Using a whisk, briskly stir in the cornmeal and stir constantly over medium heat for 2–3 minutes, or until thick. Remove and cool for 1 minute. Add the Parmesan and sage, season well with salt and pepper, and cool for another 5 minutes. Lightly flour the work surface and roll or press out the polenta to a thickness of 1/2 inch. Leave to cool and firm for 1 hour. Using a 2-inch plain cutter, cut out 25–30 disks. Place the disks in a single layer on two baking sheets lined with waxed paper and cover until needed.

2 To prepare the deviled kidneys, remove the fat and fine membrane from around the kidneys, then lay them flat, hold in place with one hand and cut each through sideways with a sharp knife. Using the tip of a sharp knife or scissors, trim away the core from the cut side of each kidney half. In a small bowl, stir together the tomato chutney, mustard, Worcestershire sauce and cayenne pepper. In a wide skillet, melt half the butter and, over a medium heat, cook the shallot for 3–4 minutes, or until golden. Transfer the shallot to a plate, wipe out the pan with paper towels and set aside.

3 Heat the oven to 250°F. Fill a deep-fat fryer or large saucepan one-third full of oil and heat to 350°F (a cube of bread dropped into the oil will brown in 15 seconds). Deep-fry the sage polenta disks in small batches for 2–3 minutes, remove from the oil and drain on crumpled paper towels. Transfer to a wire rack and keep the disks warm in the oven, uncovered so that they retain their crispness.

4 Melt the remaining butter in the skillet. When sizzling hot, add the kidneys, skin-side-down first. Cook over high heat for 20 seconds, turn over and cook for another 20 seconds. Remove to the plate with the shallot. Lower the heat, add the mustard mixture from the bowl to the pan and stir for a moment to blend. Return the kidneys and the shallot to the pan and toss for 1–2 minutes, or until cooked through. Put four or five polenta disks on each individual serving plate and divide the kidneys among them. Add the stock to the pan and cook for 1 minute, stirring to blend in the kidney juices. Pour the sauce over the kidneys and then serve immediately.

Chef's tip The deviled kidneys could be served just on toast. The sage and polenta disks would be an excellent accompaniment to serve with fried or scrambled eggs, grilled tomatoes or sautéed chicken livers.

Homemade sausage patties

These quick and easy ground pork patties can be served simply with broiled tomatoes or as part of a full traditional cooked breakfast.

Preparation time **5 minutes**
Total cooking time **4–6 minutes**
Makes 8

I teaspoon salt
1/4 teaspoon ground black pepper
pinch of fennel seeds
1/4 teaspoon paprika
3/4 lb. lean ground pork
I tablespoon oil

1 In a bowl, mix the salt, pepper, fennel and paprika with the pork. Mix in 2 tablespoons cold water. To check the seasoning, fry a little of the mixture until it is cooked through and taste it. Divide the seasoned meat into eight balls. Flatten each ball to make a patty about 1/2 inch thick.
2 Heat the oil in a skillet over medium heat. Cook the sausage patties in batches for 3–5 minutes on each side, or until browned and cooked through. Keep warm until ready to serve.

Potato griddle biscuits

These biscuits are delicious served with broiled bacon—or simply butter, jam or honey—as a leisurely brunch or breakfast.

Preparation time **10 minutes**
Total cooking time **45 minutes**
Makes 12 biscuits

3 potatoes
1/4 cup unsalted butter, at room temperature
1/2 cup all-purpose flour
I teaspoon baking powder
large pinch of grated nutmeg

1 Peel the potatoes and put them in a large saucepan of salted water. Bring to a boil, then reduce the heat and simmer until tender, approximately 30–35 minutes. Drain well, then return to the pan to dry over low heat.
2 Mash the potatoes until smooth, then beat in the butter. Sift the flour, baking powder, nutmeg and some salt into a bowl. Add the mashed potatoes and, using a round-bladed knife, knead the mixture together. You will need to use the mixture at once as baking powder is activated by moisture and warmth.
3 On a lightly floured surface, pat out the mixture to a 5/8 inch thickness. Using a 1 1/2-inch plain cutter, cut out 12 rounds. Heat a heavy-bottomed skillet or griddle over medium heat and dust lightly with flour. Cook the biscuits for about 8 minutes, or until cooked through, turning after 4 minutes. Serve warm.

Homemade sausage patties (top) and Potato griddle biscuits

Croissants

Croissants require time and effort to produce, but the rich buttery result will astound friends and family.
Served warm with jam or marmalade, they are guaranteed to disappear at an alarming rate!
On page 62 there are step-by-step illustrations showing how to make croissants.

Preparation time **3 hours + resting + chilling overnight**
Total cooking time **20 minutes**
Makes 12–16

4 cups all-purpose flour
1 teaspoon salt
3 tablespoons sugar
1¼ cups milk
¼ oz. (1 tablespoon) dried yeast
1¼ cups unsalted butter,
   at room temperature
1 egg, beaten

1 Sift the flour, salt and sugar into a large bowl and make a well in the center. Heat the milk to warm, stir in the yeast and 1 tablespoon of the flour until dissolved, then leave to stand until bubbles form. Add to the dry ingredients and mix together to make a soft dough, then turn out onto a floured work surface and knead for 5 minutes, or until smooth and elastic. Transfer the dough to a floured bowl and cover. Set aside in a warm place for about 1 hour, or until doubled in volume.

2 Meanwhile, put the butter between two sheets of plastic wrap and roll into a rectangle about 8 x 4 inches. Refrigerate until ready to use.

3 Once the dough has risen, punch it down and transfer to a floured work surface. Roll into a 16 x 5-inch rectangle. The dough should be just over twice as long as the butter and a little bit wider. Place the butter on the lower half of the dough and fold the dough over to completely enclose the butter. Seal the edges with your fingertips. Turn the dough so that the fold is on the right-hand side and lightly roll the dough into a large rectangle twice as long as it is wide. Brush off excess flour and fold the dough into even thirds like a letter, with the bottom third up and the top third down. Chill in plastic wrap for 20 minutes.

4 Remove from the refrigerator and, with the fold on the right-hand side, roll out the dough as above. Fold it as before and chill. Repeat again.

5 Remove the dough from the refrigerator and cut it in half. On a well-floured surface, roll each piece of the dough into a large rectangle, and trim it to 14½ x 8¾ inches. Using a triangular template with a base of 7 inches and sides of 5½ inches, cut the rectangle into six triangles (you should also be left with two end triangles). Roll the dough up, starting from the wide end, to form crescents. Place the croissants on baking sheets and lightly brush with the beaten egg. Cover with plastic wrap and refrigerate overnight.

6 Remove the croissants from the refrigerator and set aside to rise for about 30–45 minutes, or until doubled in size. Do not try to hurry the process by putting them anywhere too warm, or the butter in the dough will melt. Preheat the oven to 400°F.

7 Once the croissants have doubled in size, gently brush with a second layer of the beaten egg. Bake for about 15–20 minutes, or until golden brown.

Chef's tip It is very important that the dough and the butter are at the same consistency before rolling. If the butter is too soft, it will seep out as the dough is rolled, and if it is too hard, it will crack and break, leaving the final product with uneven layers. The butter should feel a little firmer than cream cheese.

Crumpets

Light and airy crumpets toasted on a fork in front of an open fire have always been a British tea-time delight, but they also make a special treat for brunch and may be toasted under the broiler or in a toaster.

Preparation time **10 minutes + 1 hour 50 minutes standing**
Total cooking time **45 minutes**
Makes 8 crumpets

1 1/2 cups milk
1/4 oz. (1 tablespoon) dried yeast
3 cups all-purpose flour
1/2 teaspoon salt
1/2 teaspoon baking soda
oil or clarified butter, for cooking

1 Pour the milk into a saucepan and heat until warm, remove from the heat and stir in the yeast.

2 Sift the flour and the salt into a bowl and make a well in the center. Pour in a little of the milk mixture and beat with a whisk, electric mixer or your hand to mix in a little of the flour to make a smooth paste. Repeat this process until all the liquid has been added and all the flour incorporated, then beat until completely smooth. Cover with a plate or plastic wrap and leave in a warm place for approximately 1–1 1/2 hours, or until doubled in size and full of bubbles. Dissolve the baking soda in 3/4 cup water. Add it to the batter and mix well. Cover and set aside for 15–20 minutes.

3 On the top of the stove, heat a griddle or a wide heavy-bottomed skillet to medium heat and brush with a little oil or clarified butter. Lightly butter or oil the inside of two or more 3 1/2–4-inch pastry cutters or crumpet rings, and put them in the pan.

4 Pour in the crumpet batter to a thickness of 1/2 inch, lower the heat to very low and cook for 7–8 minutes. The bubbles will rise as the crumpets cook. The crumpets are ready to turn over when the top has dried out enough to form a skin (see Chef's techniques, page 63). Loosen the rings, turn the crumpets over and brown the second side for 1–2 minutes. Remove and cool on a wire rack, covered with a clean towel to prevent them from drying out. Repeat with the remaining batter as the rings become free. If the batter thickens on standing, add a little more water to thin it.

5 To serve, preheat a broiler to the highest setting and toast the crumpets well on the first cooked side, then brown more lightly on the second side. Spread the lightly broiled side with butter and serve immediately.

Chef's tips If you don't have crumpet rings, you can just as easily use egg rings instead.

Fig preserves

With fabulous soft, spicy flavors of the Orient, this conserve makes a memorable accompaniment to Eastern rice pudding, or any of the sweet pancake recipes. Try a spoonful with a bowl of oatmeal.

Preparation time **10 minutes**
Total cooking time **1 hour 5 minutes**
Makes approximately 2 pints

I lemon
I lime
2 whole star anise
2 whole cloves
1 3/4 lb. fresh black, purple or green figs, stalks removed and cut into quarters
1/3 cup red wine
1 3/4 cups sugar

1 Coarsely chop the lemon and lime and place in a square of cheesecloth with the star anise and cloves. Tie into a bag, securing with string and leaving the ends long.
2 Combine the figs and red wine with 1/4 cup water in a large heavy-bottomed saucepan or kettle with a lid and tie the string of the cheesecloth bag to the pan handle, so that the bag will be suspended in the figs. Simmer gently for 15 minutes.
3 Squeeze the bag against the side of the pan with a spoon and then remove and discard. (Be careful as it will be very hot.) Stir the sugar into the mixture in the pan over low heat until the sugar dissolves.
4 Raise the heat and boil, bubbling hard, until thick and syrupy. Start checking the consistency (see Chef's techniques, page 63) from 20 minutes onwards. Continue boiling and testing for the jell stage every 5 minutes. Remember that the preserves will thicken a little more as it cools. Refrigerate and use within 2 weeks.

Kumquat preserves

Bettering a good homemade marmalade for breakfast is difficult, but this bright and zesty preserve is sure to become a favorite. Kumquats, originally native to China, are small bittersweet fruits with edible skins.

Preparation time **10 minutes + overnight standing**
Total cooking time **40 minutes**
Makes approximately 2 pints

1 1/2 lb. ripe kumquats
6 cups sugar
1/3 cup gin

1 Coarsely chop the kumquats into fairly small pieces and layer in a large bowl with the sugar. Cover and leave to stand overnight. You may, depending on the ripeness of the fruit, be able to reduce this time by an hour or so; however, the sugar should be virtually dissolved and the juice running out of the kumquats.
2 Transfer the fruits and all the sugary juices into a large heavy-bottomed saucepan or kettle and add 1 1/4 cups water. Slowly heat until any remaining sugar dissolves, stirring to prevent any of it from burning on the bottom of the pan.
3 Raise the heat and boil hard for 15–20 minutes, or until thick, but not too syrupy. Do not stir. Remove the pan from the heat, stir in the gin and test for the jell stage (see Chef's techniques, page 63). If not ready, continue boiling and testing for the jell stage every 5 minutes. Refrigerate and use within 2 weeks.

Chef's tip Kumquat seeds, unlike orange seeds, are perfectly edible when cooked, and add a delicate nuttiness to this preserve, as well as being attractive. You could, of course, pick out all the seeds as you cut up the kumquats. Then place all the seeds into a cheesecloth bag and add it to the pan with the water, removing it when the preserve has reached setting point.

Fig preserves (top) and Kumquat preserves

Scotch pancakes

These small, thick, sweet pancakes are also known as drop scones in England and are served hot and buttered with a fruity or a sweet accompaniment.

*Preparation time **8 minutes + 1 hour refrigeration***
*Total cooking time **15 minutes***
*Makes **12***

1 egg, beaten
3 tablespoons sugar
2 tablespoons unsalted butter
1¹/4 cups milk
1 cup all-purpose flour
¹/2 teaspoon baking soda
¹/2 teaspoon baking powder
¹/2 teaspoon cream of tartar

1 In a small bowl, beat the egg with half the sugar. In a small saucepan, melt the butter with the rest of the sugar. Remove from the heat and add the milk and 1 teaspoon cold water to the pan.

2 Sift together the flour, baking soda, baking powder, cream of tartar and a pinch of salt into a large bowl. Make a well in the center. Pour the egg mixture and butter mixture into the well and beat with a wooden spoon or balloon whisk until the dry ingredients have disappeared and a smooth batter is formed. Cover and refrigerate for 1 hour or overnight.

3 Brush a large nonstick skillet or griddle with melted butter and place over high heat. Using 2–3 tablespoons batter for each, drop the batter into the pan and cook for 1 minute, or until bubbles rise to the surface. Turn the pikelets over and cook for 1 minute, or until light golden. Serve immediately, or keep warm, wrapped in foil, in a 300°F oven.

Chef's tip Serve with butter, lemon juice and sugar, maple syrup or fresh fruit conserves.

Waffles

Waffles, made from a light sweetened batter, have a honeycombed surface ideal for holding large quantities of sweet runny syrup or honey for those with a particularly sweet tooth.

*Preparation time **5 minutes***
*Total cooking time **40–50 minutes***
*Makes **about 8–10 waffles***

2 cups all-purpose flour
1 tablespoon sugar
1¹/2 teaspoons baking powder
¹/2 teaspoon salt
1¹/2 cups milk or buttermilk
2 tablespoons unsalted butter, melted
2 eggs

1 Sift together the flour, sugar, baking powder and salt into a large bowl.

2 In a separate bowl, combine the milk, melted butter and eggs. Gradually add to the flour mixture and mix until blended.

3 Preheat a waffle iron according to the manufacturer's instructions. Once hot, lightly brush with oil. Pour in the recommended amount of batter and cook until golden brown in color and crispy. Serve with whipped butter and honey or maple syrup.

Scotch pancakes (top) and Waffles

Brioche

Brioche, a light yeast dough enriched with butter and eggs, is wonderful served with butter and jam for breakfast or brunch, or alternatively as an accompaniment to stewed fruit. There are many different ways to mold brioche dough—in this recipe it has been molded into the traditional brioche à tête, *where the small ball on the top represents the "head" of the brioche. See page 62 for step-by-step instructions.*

*Preparation time **30 minutes + 4 hours rising***
*Total cooking time **25 minutes***
Makes 1 large loaf or 4 small loaves

3 tablespoons warm milk
1/4 oz. (1 tablespoon) dried yeast
3 cups bread or all-purpose flour
1/4 cup sugar
1 teaspoon salt
6 eggs, lightly beaten
3/4 cup unsalted butter, at room temperature
1 egg, beaten and mixed with 2 tablespoons of water, for glazing

1 Pour the milk into a bowl and dissolve the yeast in it. Add 1 tablespoon of the flour, cover and set aside until bubbles start to appear. Sift the remaining flour, sugar and salt into a large bowl, make a well in the center and add the beaten eggs and yeast mixture. Gradually mix the flour into the wet ingredients to make a sticky dough, then transfer to a floured surface.
2 Lift and throw the dough down on the work surface with floured hands for 20 minutes, or until the dough forms a smooth ball. Place in an oiled bowl and turn the dough over to coat with the oil. Cover and let rise at room temperature for 2–21/2 hours, or until doubled in volume.
3 Turn out the dough, punch down, cover and leave to rest for 5 minutes, then transfer to the work surface again. Place the soft butter on top of the dough and pinch and squeeze the two of them together until they are well combined. Knead for 5 more minutes, or until the dough is smooth again. Cover and let rest for 5 minutes.
4 Brush a 5-cup brioche mold or four small 2-cup brioche molds liberally with melted butter. If using the small molds, divide the dough into four pieces. Set aside a quarter of each piece of dough. Shape the large pieces into balls and drop them into the molds seam-side-down. Make a hole in the top of each ball using your finger and shape the reserved pieces into tear-drop shapes to fit into the holes. Press down to seal. Cover and leave to rise for 1–11/2 hours, or until the molds are half to three-quarters full. Preheat the oven to 400°F. Lightly brush with the egg glaze and bake for 20–25 minutes, or until a nice golden brown. Turn out and allow to cool on a wire rack.

Chef's tip To make raisin brioche, simply soak 2 tablespoons chopped raisins in some rum to plump them up. Drain and add to the dough after the butter has been incorporated.

Sour cherry pecan bread

*If dried sour cherries or muscatels are difficult to
obtain, coarsely chopped dried apricots may
be substituted, just as hazelnuts may be
used in place of the pecans.*

Preparation time **10 minutes**
Total cooking time **1 hour 5 minutes**
Serves **6–8**

1/2 cup sugar
1/2 cup golden syrup or dark corn syrup
I cup milk
I egg, beaten
2 cups all-purpose flour
I teaspoon ground cinnamon
I tablespoon baking powder
1/3 cup dried sour cherries, chopped, or
   muscatel raisins
1/2 cup coarsely chopped pecans

1 Brush a 9 x 5 x 3-inch loaf pan with melted butter
and line with foil, letting it hang over the two longest
sides. Preheat the oven to 350°F.
2 In a small saucepan over low heat, warm the sugar,
syrup and milk and stir until the sugar dissolves.
Remove from the heat and set aside to cool to
lukewarm. Stir in the egg.
3 Sift the flour, cinnamon, baking powder and a pinch
of salt into a bowl and toss in the sour cherries or raisins
and pecans. Add the syrup mixture and stir quickly until
all the ingredients are just combined. Pour immediately
into the loaf pan and bake for 1 hour. (Cover loosely
with foil after 30 minutes if the bread appears to be
browning too quickly.) The bread will be done when the
surface springs back when pressed with your fingertips.
4 Leave to cool for 10 minutes, then turn out onto a
wire rack. The bread improves with keeping and can be
stored, wrapped in plastic wrap or foil, for up to 2 weeks
in a cool place. Serve plain or buttered.

Danish pastries

Although this recipe may be time-consuming, nothing quite matches the taste of this freshly made,
rich and flaky yeast dough.

Preparation time **3 hours + refrigeration**
Total cooking time **30 minutes**
Makes 28

8 cups bread or all-purpose flour
1/3 cup sugar
4 teaspoons salt
1/2 oz. (2 tablespoons) dried yeast
3 cups warm milk
1 3/4 cups unsalted butter,
  chilled
1 egg, beaten
1/2 cup sliced almonds
confectioners' sugar, to dust

PASSIONFRUIT CREAM FILLING
2 tablespoons sugar
2 large egg yolks
2 teaspoons all-purpose flour
2 teaspoons cornstarch
1/2 cup passionfruit juice or pulp

OR

ORANGE CREAM FILLING
2 tablespoons sugar
2 large egg yolks
2 teaspoons all-purpose flour
2 teaspoons cornstarch
1/2 cup orange juice

1 Grease and flour a baking sheet. Sift the flour, sugar and salt into a large bowl and make a well in the center. Cream the yeast with 3 tablespoons of the milk. Stir in the remaining milk and pour into the well in the dry ingredients. Gradually mix in the flour with your fingers until the mixture makes a soft dough. Knead the dough on a floured surface until it is smooth and elastic. Cover with plastic wrap in a bowl and chill for 10 minutes.

2 To make the passionfruit cream filling, place the sugar, egg yolks, flour and cornstarch in a medium bowl and mix well. Bring the juice to a boil in a medium saucepan. Add a little to the sugar mixture, stir to blend, then add the sugar mixture to the saucepan. Bring the mixture to a boil, stirring constantly, and cook for 1 minute. Cover and leave to cool.

3 To make the orange cream filling, proceed exactly as for the passionfruit filling above, using the orange juice instead of the passionfruit juice or pulp.

4 On a floured surface, roll out the dough into a rectangle three times as long as it is wide, and 1/8 inch thick. Tap and roll out the butter within two long sheets of plastic wrap into a rectangle, the same width as, but two thirds the length of, the dough. Unwrap and lay the butter on the top two thirds of the dough. Fold the exposed third of the dough up over the butter and fold the top third down.

5 Turn the dough to look like a book, with the binding on the left, and roll again into a rectangle and fold into three layers. Repeat twice, wrapping in plastic wrap and chilling for 20 minutes between each roll.

6 On a floured surface, roll the dough into an 1/8-inch thick square or rectangle. Cut into 5 x 4-inch rectangles and place on the baking sheet.

7 To make the Danish pastries, preheat the oven to 400°F. Spoon the filling into a pastry bag and pipe into the center of each pastry. Bring up the corners and press together firmly. Set aside in a warm place to proof for 30 minutes. Brush with the egg, avoiding the sides of the pastry because this will prevent the dough from rising as it cooks. Sprinkle with a few sliced almonds and bake for 15–20 minutes, or until golden. Cool on wire racks and dust with sifted confectioners' sugar, if desired.

Red fruit preserves

This dark red fruit preserves is simply delicious served with buttered toast, brioche, waffles or used as a filling in crêpes.

Preparation time **5 minutes**
Total cooking time **1 hour 30 minutes**
Makes about 1½ pints

2 lb. mixed fresh or frozen soft red fruits
8 cups sugar

1 Combine the fruit and sugar with 1/4 cup water in a large saucepan or kettle and slowly heat for 4 minutes, or until the sugar has dissolved, stirring to prevent the sugar burning onto the bottom of the pan. Place two or three saucers or small plates in the freezer.
2 Raise the heat and boil rapidly until syrupy and jam-like in consistency. Skim off any scum that forms on the surface. The cooking may take from 30 minutes to 1½ hours, depending on the acidity in your choice of fruits. Start checking for consistency after 30 minutes, by drawing a spoon through the mixture to see if it

"parts." If it does, pick up a little of the mixture on the spoon and tip it to the side. If it falls in heavy drops from the spoon, it is ready for the final test. To do the final test on the preserves, put a teaspoon of the mixture on one of the cold saucers, allow to cool slightly and press lightly forward with your index finger. If the jell stage is reached, the preserves should have a slight skin, which will wrinkle as you press. Also, if you draw your finger through the preserves it will stay separated and not run back together (see Chef's techniques, page 63). If the mixture is not ready, reboil it, testing it every 5 minutes until it is. Do not overboil or the fruit will lose its color and have a caramelized flavor.
3 When ready, remove from the heat and cool. Stir again to disperse the fruit and then spoon into clean bowls or sterilized jars. Seal and process jars in a water-bath canner according to the manufacturers' instructions, or seal with melted paraffin and cool, then store in the refrigerator until used.

Chef's techniques

◆

Croissants

Folding the butter into the dough and refolding creates layers that puff up when cooked.

When the dough has risen, punch it down, then roll it out to a rectangle just over twice as long as the butter and a little wider. Put the butter on the lower half of the dough and bring the dough over to enclose it.

Turn the dough so the fold is on the right, then roll out into a rectangle. Fold the dough into three even layers, like a letter, with the bottom third up and the top third down. Chill, then repeat twice.

Cut the dough in half and roll out into two large rectangles. Using a triangular template, cut the rectangles into six triangles (you will be left with the two end pieces).

Roll the triangles from the wide end, to shape crescents.

Brioche

Brioche dough is not as firm as bread dough and the butter needs to be beaten in.

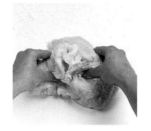

Lightly flour your hands and lift and throw the dough down on a work surface for about 20 minutes, or until the dough forms a smooth ball.

After the dough has risen, punch it down, cover and leave it for 5 minutes. Transfer it to the work surface and blend in the butter, pinching and squeezing the two of them together until well combined.

Knead for 5 minutes, or until the dough is very smooth.

Shape the large pieces of dough into balls and drop them into the molds seam-side-down. Make a hole in the top with your finger and fit the small tear-drop pieces of dough into the holes. Press down to seal.

Bagels

The secret to making bagels is the process of boiling before baking, creating the chewy texture.

Roll the dough into tight balls, poke your finger through the center of each ball and gently enlarge the hole until the dough resembles a doughnut.

Cook the bagels in simmering water for 1 minute each side.

Brush the bagels with beaten egg before baking for 20–25 minutes. They can be sprinkled with poppy or sesame seeds before baking.

Hollandaise sauce

This sauce must not be allowed to get too hot, otherwise it may curdle.

Whisk the egg yolks and water together in a heatproof bowl until foamy. Place the bowl over a pan half-filled with simmering water and whisk until thick. The bowl should not touch the water. Gradually whisk in the butter.

Continue adding the melted butter, over very low heat, whisking constantly. The sauce should leave a trail on the surface when the whisk is lifted.

Once all the butter is incorporated, strain the sauce into a clean bowl, stir in the lemon juice and then season with salt and pepper.

Crumpets

Crumpets are delicious when freshly made at home and are not difficult to make.

Cook the crumpets until bubbles appear. They are ready to turn over when the top has dried out enough to form a skin.

Testing fruit preserves

When testing for the jell stage, use a saucer that has been in the freezer or refrigerator.

Put a teaspoon of the mixture on the cold saucer. The preserves should form a slight skin that will wrinkle when you pass your index finger through it.

First published in the United States in 1998 by Periplus Editions (HK) Ltd., with editorial offices at
153 Milk Street, Boston, Massachusetts 02109.

Murdoch Books and Le Cordon Bleu thank the 32 masterchefs of all the Le Cordon Bleu Schools, whose knowledge and
expertise have made this book possible, especially: Chef Cliche (MOF), Chef Terrien, Chef Boucheret, Chef Duchêne (MOF),
Chef Guillut, Chef Steneck, Paris; Chef Males, Chef Walsh, Chef Hardy, London; Chef Chantefort, Chef Bertin, Chef Jambert,
Chef Honda, Tokyo; Chef Salembien, Chef Boutin, Chef Harris, Sydney; Chef Lawes, Adelaide; Chef Guiet, Chef Denis, Ottawa.
Of the many students who helped the Chefs test each recipe, a special mention to graduates David Welch and Allen Wertheim.
A very special acknowledgment to Directors Susan Eckstein, Great Britain, and Kathy Shaw, Paris, who have been responsible for
the coordination of the Le Cordon Bleu team throughout this series.

The Publisher and Le Cordon Bleu also wish to thank Carole Sweetnam for her help with this series.

First published in Australia in 1998 by Murdoch Books®

Managing Editor: Kay Halsey
Series Concept, Design and Art Direction: Juliet Cohen
Editor: Wendy Stephen
Food Director: Jody Vassallo
Food Editors: Lulu Grimes, Tracy Rutherford
US Editor: Linda Venturoni Wilson
Designer: Annette Fitzgerald
Photographers: Joe Filshie, Chris Jones, Luis Martin
Food Stylists: Carolyn Fienberg, Mary Harris
Food Preparation: Jo Forrest, Alison Turner, Kerrie Mullins
Chef's Techniques Photographer: Reg Morrison
Home Economists: Anna Beaumont, Michelle Lawton, Justine Poole, Kerrie Ray, Margot Smithyman

Library of Congress catalog card number: 98-85725
ISBN 962-593-449-9

Front cover: Rösti with bacon

Distributed in the United States by
Charles E. Tuttle Co., Inc.
RR1 Box 231-5
North Clarendon, VT 05759
Tel: (802) 773-8930
Fax: (802) 773-6993

PRINTED IN SINGAPORE

05 04 03 02 01 00 99 98 10 9 8 7 6 5 4 3 2 1

Important: Some of the recipes in this book may include raw eggs, which can cause salmonella poisoning.
Those who might be at risk from this (the elderly, pregnant women, young children and those suffering
from immune deficiency diseases) should check with their physicians before eating raw eggs.